cHArminG HoteLs

CITY • COUNTRY • SEA

CHArMING HOTELS

CITY • COUNTRY • SEA

WATSON
GUPTILL

Author
Francisco Asensio Cerver

Editorial director
Paco Asensio

Design
Mireia Casanovas Soley

Layout
Jeroni Roca

Project coordinator and texts
Anna Tiessler

Translation and copy editing
Michael Webb

Photographers
Francisco Po Egea (*The Sloane, Parador de Granada, Schloss Vier Jahreszeiten, The Lowell, The Hiragiya-Ryokan, Seteais Palace, Villa San Michele, Réaux Hotel, Hacienda Benazuza, Guanahani Hotel, K. Club, Bora Bora Lagoon Resort, Regent Beverly Whilshire*)

Relais Châteaux (*Château Tour des Puits, The Point, Château Roumégouse, El Castell, Les Terrasses*)

Pere Planells (*Saignon Hotel, L'Hostalet 1701, Château Plessis, Las Brisas Hotel*)

Cookie Kinkead (*Hacienda Katanchel*)

Copyright
© 1999 - Francisco Asensio Cerver

ISBN
0-8230-0618-2

DLB:
B-31.685-1999

Printed in Spain
Cayfosa Indústria Gràfica
Santa Perpètua de la Mogoda. Barcelona

First published in 1999 by **arco** for Hearst Books International, an imprint of Harper Collins
1350 Avenue of the Americas
New York, NY 10019

Distributed in the U.S. and Canada by
Watson-Guptill Publications
1515 Broadway
New York, NY 10036

Distributed throughout the rest of the world by
Hearst Books International, an imprint of Harper Collins
1350 Avenue of the Americas
New York, NY 10019

Introduction

cHArM

Although the term charming expresses a feeling that is quite subjective, observers nevertheless often agree when objects, ambiences, or situations are charming. In order to achieve this feeling, a series of distinct aspects must obviously be brought to such a level of perfection that their total impact rises above what each of these aspects might inspire separately. In the case of hotels, charm derives not only from the style of the building, the suitability of the decor, and the excellence of the service, it also derives from the overall impact of these characteristics, as well as from certain less definable qualities such as the pleasantness of the surroundings, and the imaginativeness and personability of the hotel's execution.

This book presents a carefully chosen selection of twenty-seven hotels that are indisputably charming. These each have a unique flavor and an ambience that is meaningful to nearly any observer. Charm is not the only quality that these hotels have in common, however.

All adhere to the highest standards of professionalism. Having paid such meticulous attention to providing a personal touch, these hotels lie well outside the mainstream of the hospitality industry.

We have divided the hotels into three groups according to whether the hotels are in an urban, rural, or coastal setting. By dividing the hotels into these groups, we are reaffirming the basic principle which says that decorative and architectural solutions used in hotels must respond as specifically as possible to the particular needs of the guests themselves. This division leaves intact the individual personalities of the hotels, because in each chapter we find solutions that are unique.

In the urban group, for example, we find hotels as diverse as the Lowell, the Hiragiya Ryokan, the Parador de Granada, and the Sloane, among others. The Lowell, on New York's Upper East Side, is the epitome of the classic urban American hotel, with a stern and respectful demeanor typified by its eighteenth and nineteenth century engravings. This demeanor has been preserved even during recent renovations. The Hiragiya Ryokan in Tokyo provides another important reference point, with its exquisite interior design based on folding screens, gold leaf, Zen-inspired painted papers, and lacquers. In contrast, the magic of the Parador lies in its synthesis of Christian and Arab cultures, as exemplified by its austere, monastic stonework made more refined by the delicate coloring of the Arab tiling. Finally, in the heart of London we find the exalted Victorian style, making the Sloane an irresistible temptation for our collection.

The hotels featured in this book belong to categories that are best

iNg HoteLs

described by giving several well-defined examples of each. This is true not only for the hotels in the urban category, but also for those in the rural and coastal categories. Villa San Michele, for example, which is in the heart of the Tuscan countryside, was born as a rugged Franciscan monastery, and many of its attractive qualities are due to the survival of the original chapels, cloisters, and inner patios. The Roumégouse Château, in the French Lot region, is a fanciful, nineteenth century Neogothic building. Its decoration is almost worthy of a museum, since each well-maintained piece of furniture is an original. Good French taste keeps this weighty legacy from feeling oppressive, however.

Formerly belonging to the Rockefeller family, the Point is a magnificent enhancement to its beautiful natural setting. Its rooms are distributed in several separate sections along the bank of Lake Saranac in an Adirondack forest. In a completely different setting and with other architectural and decorative styles, we find the Hacienda Benazuza. This hotel is set amidst Arab-Andalusian gardens 15 minutes from Seville, in an oasis surrounded by mature olive trees and by buildings with intense colors, such as traditional limestone white, ochre red, and a vivid yellow.

Although many of the buildings with artistic merit that are found in the city and the countryside are historical, the same is not necessarily true of hotels along the coast. The hotels featured in the third section are often completely new buildings, conceived to fit into and take advantage of the cliffs, rocks, and sand of their coastal environment. In this section we present several examples of fine hotels from the Mediterranean region along with several from the Caribbean, such as the Guanahani, Jacke's Place, Jamaica Inn, and the K Club.

All of these hotels are extraordinary. Jamaica Inn has long been a local favorite, but it has also hosted such famous international guests as Sir Winston Churchill and Errol Flynn. The K Club in Barbados is a tranquil paradise on a deserted beach near a nature reserve. Jacke's Place is in Treasure Beach, a Jamaican fishing village. The rooms of Jack's Place are individual cabins, giving the hotel a flavor of the local buildings. The Guanahani is an intimate hotel on the island of Saint Barthélemy. It has been designed to be as open as possible to its breathtakingly beautiful surroundings, which include tamarinds, palms, and coconuts, the lush tropical gardens, the intense blue of the water, and the nearby corral reefs.

The hotels featured in this collection are all exceptional for their rare charm and warm elegance.

city Hotels

the Sloane

Chelsea, London, UK

The Sloane is a small and intimate hotel located in the heart of London in a Victorian mansion. The hotel is near one of the most highly coveted commercial zones and has easy access to London's financial district, the City. This fact determines the hotel's orientation. Most of its regular guests are high-level executives and the services offered by the hotel are expressly conceived for them. This even extends to the food offered, which emphasizes a healthy diet.

However, efficiency does not disdain the imagination. The Sloane is an establishment that shows striking personality in its decor. The twelve rooms have been individually designed with originality and even with a sense of fantasy. Even the smallest piece of furniture merits attention: thick brocades, smooth silks, upholstery with gentle tones, delicate cushions with antique cases, art objects of every style, from the most Victorian to the purely Neoclassical. All this is an active exercise in eclecticism that holds many surprises. Its formula seems to be to achieve maximum comfort with the greatest originality. Guests may enjoy a broad view of Chelsea from a terrace on the upper floor in a room where receptions are held. This is the perfect space for the English custom of taking tea, and is also a delightful place for having breakfast, lunches, or cocktails.

Each room has enough space for the guests to feel at home, with a specific space for relaxation. The guests are afforded maximum privacy, both in the rooms and in the central business services area. The superlative respect given by English service, the atmosphere of choice antiques, and the Victorian mansion itself all complement the unique combination of services offered by the Sloane.

Plan view of the entrance with its wooden stairs.

Detail of one of the sitting rooms in the hotel.

The guest rooms are decorated with thick brocades and gentle tones.

Detail of silver service.

The interior decor of the bedrooms have a distinct Victorian flavor.

Suite with fabrics that have coordinated shades in flowers and cashmere.

The beds have elaborate canopies.

parador de granada

Granada, Spain

The Parador of Granada is located within an enclosed space in the Alhambra, next to the Palace of Charles the Fifth and the Alcázar. The building was originally the palace of an Arab prince, and its first reconstruction took place during the reign of Yusuf the First in the fifteenth century. The Catholic Monarchs intended it to be used as a Franciscan convent after the Christian reconquest, and it became a perfect example of the synthesis of the exuberant Arabic style of ornamentation and the sober architectural lines of the Castilian Renaissance. In 1945 it was inaugurated as a parador, after a suitable adaptation of its surroundings, and the last renovations took place in 1992 and 1996. The rooms, baths, and communal areas of the cloister were remodeled under the direction of the architect Carlos Fernández Carabantes, who recovered the remaining original furniture and gradually added hand polychromies based on Mudejar techniques. The restoration of the furnishings in the remaining rooms is planned to take place in 1999 according to the same criteria.

The sobriety of the convent style has been made more subtle by the use of color in the Arabic tiles, by the abundance of flowers, and by the endless murmuring of running water. These elements serve as a reminder that the architecture of Granada was originally conceived by the Arabic calyphs as an immense garden. The result is a peaceful and magical place allowing one to enjoy almost complete solitude even though the hotel is in the midst of a city. All that is necessary to realize that Granada has a very special character is to sit quietly on the terrace adjacent to the dining room, with the Albaycín and Sacromonte on the horizon and the babbling of fountains and chirping of birds. The rooms of the Parador are different and all are exterior. Some have a terrace. Through the windows, guests enjoy a view of the Generalife, the Albaycín, and the glorious magic of Granada.

Detail of an antique door with a gold latch.

Behind the door the charm of this place is visible, endlessly evoking its Arabic past.

The interior gardens remind us that this place was also once a Franciscan convent.

Next to the cloister, old wooden benches allow guests to take in the soothing and magical atmosphere.

In the center of the ancient cloister, a small fountain surrounded by fruit trees, plants, and teak furniture.

Detail of the interior furnishings of the Parador.

On warm days the wooden shutters filter the light in the interior spaces.

Detail of the altar of the chapel decorated with Baroque lines.

View of the mountains of Granada from one of the rooms. In the foreground, antique Spanish furniture can be seen.

The dining room, with its full views of the outside, is decorated with a profusion of textiles with floral designs.

Each room of the Parador is set apart by its antiques. A wood carving on a chest. In the foreground can be seen an armchair and small side table for reading and resting.

SCHLOSS VIER JAHRESZEITEN

Berlin, Germany

Located in the center of Berlin, the Hotel Schloss Vierjahreszeiten was built in 1912 as a private mansion of Emperor Wilhelm's doctor, W. Pannitz. Between 1992 and 1996 the building was totally remodeled and redecorated. The restoration preserved the original design and also recovered the original work that had been done by master stucco artisans who worked with gold leaf. Some elements such as the teardrop lamps were salvaged. The antiques in the hotel were found in auction houses throughout Europe.

The artistic oversight and the interior design was carried out by Karl Lagerfeld. There is not a single furnishing, mirror, or rug that has not been proposed by that well known fashion designer, including the marvelous signet and the letterhead of the hotel, the design of the table service, the menus, and the Muscadet wine that is served exclusively in the Vivaldi restaurant.

The lobby is decorated in a Renaissance Italian style with an impressive ceiling that features a coffered grid. The other rooms are done in French style, and the library has ceilings painted by hand.

The hotel has 40 rooms, 12 suites, and Karl Lagerfeld's apartment-suite is also available to guests. This space has been uniquely decorated with furniture from Lagerfeld's private residences in Paris, Monaco, and Brittany.

The Roman design of the pool is also noteworthy. The hotel offers services such as a sauna, a fitness center, and direct access to the garden.

The hotel has unequivocably become an obligatory reference for international tourism.

The impressive coffered-grid ceiling of the lobby is in Neoclassical style.

Detail of hotel furniture. A bronze and gold clock flanked by a pair of candelabras sits on an antique console.

The exclusive bar, Le Tire Bouchon, is decorated in a purely English style with an antique fireplace and wood paneling on the ceiling.

Karl Lagerfeld's apartment-suite. The great creator of fashion and design brought his private painter from Paris in order to decorate the walls of his bedroom with a frieze based on a design by André Dubreuil. The vases are by Borek Sipatz and the armchairs by Joseph Hoffman. The bed is covered with velvet that has an antique-pink tone.

Bath of the suite, showing its blue tones. The hand basin is marble.

The colors olive-green and almond prevail in the sitting room. The sofas and chairs, covered in velvet, have been designed by Dagobert Pesche. The walls are decorated with various early twentieth century motifs.

The mirror room is a dining room for banquets and other events.

Room in one of the hotel suites, with noteworthy antiques and Persian rugs.

An impressive marble fireplace presides over this space, which is suitable for relaxing and reading.

Bedroom with a Gustavian sense, and in which blues and whites predominate.

the LoWeLL

New York, USA

The Lowell is an architecturally significant building. Located in the Upper
East Side, it has been recommended for listing in the National Register
of Historical Places. Designed by Henry Stern Churchill, The Lowell Hotel
was constructed in 1925 as an apartment hotel with a first floor
restaurant and lobby. Its Art Decó facade is a distinguished design in
brick and terracotta, integrating a richly decorated floor entrance and
upper floors. The Lowell acts as an important streetscape feature in its
block, which combines late nineteen and early twentieth town houses
with larger twentieth century apartment buildings in the harmonious
fashion that typifies the area. As when it originally opened its doors,
The Lowell still is an intimate, confortable hotel.

One might think that this landmark building, situated on a peaceful
treelined street is in the heart of Paris. The Lowell Hotel, however, is
located in Manhattan's Upper East Side, between Madison and Park
Avenue, steps away from Manhattan's famous museums and New York
City's World renowned Madison and Fifth Avenue boutiques and shops.
From the architecture to the service, this charming hotel reflects an
European elegance.

A liveried doorman ushers the guest to an Empire Style reception desk with
no registration lines. The "hotel intime" atmosphere is complete with
lobby designed by Dalmar Tift III which combines Art Decó touches,
French Empire Style furniture with lustrous golden scalamandres,
chiaroscuro walls and a rare desk console signed by Edgar Brandt.
The lobby is contiguous to the famous Post House Restaurant from
which its entrance is separated by an original 1920's door.

The management, who is highly respectful of their elite customers'
privacy, run this New-European haven like a "Pied-a-terre", a home
away from home. Each room has been uniquely decorated: Eighteenth
and Nineteenth Century prints, Chinese porcelains, wood burning
fireplaces, libraries, full service kitchens and marble baths with brass
fixtures complete the elegance offered in these confortable rooms,
some of them with private terraces.

The Lowell recently unveiled its "Gym Suite", a one-bedroom space which
includes a fully equipped room with a breathtaking view of Manhattan.
The Lowell also recently opened their unique "Hollywood Suite" which
pays tribute to the Hollywood of the 1930's and boasts a conference
and meeting room with the latest state of the art equipment.

Designed with the fitness enthusiast in mind, the Gym Suite with his and her bathrooms is unique to The Lowell hotel.

The Lowell hotel combines the atmosphere of a European retreat with the warmth and familiarity of home. With its heritage charming service, The Lowell has perfected a standard of excellence which remains the hotel's hallmark among the world's travellers.

The Lowell's rooms provide guests with the perfect setting for afternoon tea, coffee or cognac. Wood burning fireplaces, refined antiques, fresh flowers, and a library of books highlight each room's character.

Nestled in a serene setting on the second floor, The Pembroke Room is identified only by discreet letters etched on the frosted glass and mahogany doors. Breakfast, weekend brunch or afternoon tea are regally presented on hand painted china.

The rooms are an example of the hotel's immaculate attention to detail. The room's decor embodies and old-world charm.

Accomodations are outfitted with mini bars and snacks, home entertainment centers, television and air conditioning.

The rich tones found in the penthouse are enhanced by the warm of a wood burning fire and cooled by a series of terraced gardens. Overlooking picturesque Manhattan, guests relax on one of the many terraces adorning Lowell rooms.

the Hiragiya-Ryokan

Kyoto, Japan

The Kyoto Hiragiya Hotel opened its doors in 1818 and in the 150 years
since then has acquired a tremendous reputation as one of the most
traditional hotels in Japan. It takes its name from a species of holly
(hiiragi) which is considered to bring good luck. The hotel was
remodeled in recent years with exemplary minimalist Japanese decor,
combining Japanese tradition with Western notions of convenience.
The bedrooms are exquisitely designed, each with a unique motif from
the repertoire of typical Japanese details. Examples of these
characteristic details are gold leaf folding screens, paper screens
painted in Zen style, beams of polished wood, lacquers used
throughout (including in the bathrooms), carved lintels, and antique,
lacquer and nacre-encrusted secretary desks. These details combined
remind us of the distinct style of ancient Japan, characterized by the
almost total absence of furnishings and by tatami mats, sliding
fusuma doors, and windows with panels of shoji paper.
The tolonoma, or bedroom, is also defined by the harmonious and
deliberate placement of porcelains and highly interesting art objects.
In order to preserve the floor rugs, Japanese people customarily remove
their shoes upon entering a home. This ritual is also observed in
Hotel Hiragiya. Another traditional Japanese habit that is observed
here is the community bath.
All the interior rooms, both private and common, are designed with
natural materials such as silk, clay, rice paper, ceramic, or sand, with
earth colors predominating in contrast to the dark tones of the
lacquered furniture.
The hotel has a typically Japanese garden inhabited by native species of
plants. Scattered throughout the garden are small fountains and
gravel paths, making the element of water the centerpiece of the
design. A hotel restaurant offers fine Kaiseki cuisine in Kyoto style,
served in handmade Kiyomizu ceramic or on fine porcelain dishes.

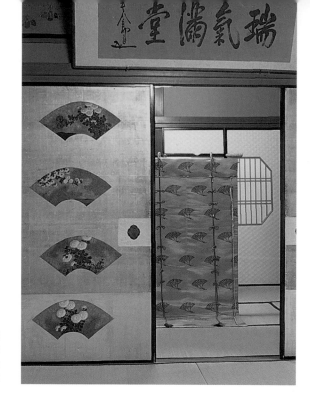

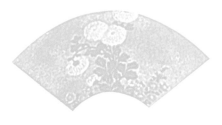

The sliding fusuma doors decorated with traditional motifs allow for effective creation of larger spaces and for convenient passage from one room to another.

A simple wooden shelf holds a blue porcelain vase and a small wooden sculpture. A mural painting graces the wall.

The small tatami mats are an ever-present element in Japanese interiors. In this roomy suite, sliding door panels serve to partition the space. At one end, next to the garden, a large salon with natural-colored sofas and a small auxiliary wardrobe.

A tray with fine porcelain, prepared for the Tea Ceremony.

A dresser with portable mirrors and drawers seems to enlarge a corner of the bedroom that is also furnished with mats and rice paper panels.

Lacquered trays for holding papers and correspondence.

The hotel's inner garden has a definite Japanese style. Immediately noticeable are the small bamboo fountain, the gravel paths, and the intensely green vegetation.

the ʃan roque

Tenerife, Canary Islands, Spain

The traditional architecture of the Canaries represents a fascinating bridge between the colonial architecture of South America and Spanish architecture in the fifteenth and sixteenth centuries. Broad halls, a large plant-filled interior patio, an upper gallery, and tiny wood carvings all combine in Hotel San Roque to create a striking overall impression. The hotel has been established in a seventeenth-century house that offers two surprises at first glance. The first is the reddish tone of the facade, which contrasts with the bright white that prevails in Garachico. The second surprise is the furniture, which amounts to an instructive display of the birth of modern design. Here one finds furniture and decor that encompass everything from the pure Art Nouveau of Mackintosh to Le Corbusier, passing through Hoffmann, Rietveld, Van der Rohe, Grey, Eckart Muthesius, and various designers connected to the Bauhaus. Without contrast, the original structure of the house gracefully accommodates choices realized by the interior designer Luis Adelantado.

Contrasting with the black volcanic sand beaches and basaltic cliffs of the coast is the laurelwood forest of the Monte del Agua and the Teno wilderness park full of native species. This is the framework in which Hotel San Roque offers a range of activities to its guests. These activities include everything from hikes to fishing and diving.

The rooms of the hotel are ideal for resting. Efforts have been taken to give each room a unique personality, always with an eye toward making sure that the furnishings are relevant in terms of the history of design. Each room has its own sound system with a full collection of CDs, along with the usual services such as satellite TV and a jacuzzi. The hotel has two bars, one of which is on a patio, and the other in a restaurant, called the Anturium, which specializes in maintaining the best traditions of Canary cuisine with fish dishes playing a major role.

View of the interior of the hotel, shows a well-lit patio decorated with designer furniture.

Main facade.

Enormous clay flower pots frame one of the arcades of the lower floor.

Large windows have been covered with loop curtains that soften the light.

The arched wooden roof and the parquet floor add a warm, rustic touch to this room.

Sober decor defines each of the rooms.

ſeteaiſ palace

Sintra, Portugal

Seteais Palace is in Sintra, which is one of the most beautiful cities in
Portugal, and the palace itself deserves its place in the guidebook as
one of the attractions of the city. The palace was built in the
eighteenth century by the Dutch consul Daniel Goldmeester. Later it
was sold to the Marquis of Marialva, who enlarged it in 1802 with
the addition of a second section. This section is tied to the main
section by an arch that is crowned by a coat of arms showing the
figures of João IV and his wife. Designed in Neoclassical style, the
palace has a French garden, two tennis courts, a swimming pool, and
a magnificent esplanade for sunbathing. The hotel is located at the
foot of the lush Montserrate Sierra, and from there guests may
enjoy beautiful views of the Atlantic beaches and the area around
Cabo Roca.

The palace was renovated and redecorated in 1994. The Neoclassical
tradition was preserved, however, and the palace recalls buildings
from the eighteenth century and the beginnings of the nineteenth.
The interior has features that show off the spaciousness of the hotel,
such as broad staircases, large paintings, decorated ceilings, and
exquisite furnishings, all of which help to define the rooms of the
hotel, including the restaurant and the Oval Hall.

The sitting rooms have walls and ceilings painted with floral period
motifs. Large drapes frame and adorn the windows. Persian rugs,
antiques, and teardrop crystal lamps take us back to the time of
lavish parties organized by the Marquis of Marialva.

The hotel has thirty rooms and three suites that have all been tastefully
decorated. The stencils of garlands and rosettes on the walls are
especially noteworthy. The grounds of the palace evoke a sense of
French influence. The layout of the gardens, features a terrace and a
separate area for horseback riding. According to local myth, the
setting of the grounds is so tranquil that one can still hear the
distant echo of the seven sighs of the princess who was the
namesake and legend behind this extraordinary hotel.

Detail of the garden.

*Seteais is elegantly
decorated in an
eighteenth century style.*

View of one of the sitting rooms.

The walls of the hotel are decorated with fresco paintings and stucco.

On the following page:
dining room with views
of the garden.

Detail of one of the suites.

The rooms are spacious
and have numerous
antiques.

*Private dining room based around a vaguely
Gustavian-style table and chairs.*

*The art of the table is an absolute
requirement in Seteais Palace.*

*The wood contrasts with the
profusely adorned fabrics.*

A fireplace is the center of attention in this room.

regent beverly wilshire

Los Angeles, USA

Eventhough it is obvious that this hotel is not the best example of a "Charming Hotel", it was decided to finally include it as a representation of the American classical hotel. Not until 1928 did the city acquire its sophistication and personality. For that year marked the arrival of the Beverly Wilshire Apartment Hotel with its unrivaled Italian Renaissance style and French neoclassic influence.

Facing Rodeo Drive and the Hollywood Hills, the Regent Beverly Wilshire is situated where every visitor to Los Angeles wants to be: a stroll away from the world's most exclusive shops, galleries and restaurants, surrounded by the stars, with a convenience distance from everything from the airport to the studios to the Pacific. It has spacious rooms and bath, four award-winning all-day choices for dining, refreshment or entertainment and the facilities for some of the finest presentations and events in Los Angeles, the pampering of a complete health spa and finally, the service for which The Regent is world renowned. " At any hour of any day, room service is at your call".

The hotel is also famous for having the most gracious lobby in all of Beverly Hills. An eloquent introduction: classically vaulted and pillared, in glowing with marble, mahogany, brass, the Grand Lobby reflects the 1928 grandeur befitting, an impression reinforced by every entryway.

The courteous service at the Wilshire Regent makes guests feel welcome and comfortable.

The sense of luxury that defines this hotel is exemplified by the classical and exquisite decor of the dining room.

The furniture is basically classical and creates a warm but sophisticated atmosphere for the entire space.

Detail of one of the rooms that offers a fireplace

The washroom facilities combine strictly functional elements with objects that are decorative and entertaining.

country hotels

Hotel ferme de la renÇonnière

Crépon, France

Hotel Ferme de la Rençonnière, a charming forty-two-room hotel, is in a peaceful country setting near Crépon near the Norman coast. It is an aristocratic residence dating from the thirteenth and fifteenth centuries with an annex called "La Ferme de Mathan" that has been an ancestral home since the eighteenth century.

La Ferme de la Rençonnière serves as a reference point for all establishments that are based on traditional local gastronomy, an attractive environment, and the range and quiet comfort of hotel services. The building is made of a solid, raw stone ashlar, which corresponds to the historical use of this building as a fortification, as a center of farm production, and as a residence for aristocrats, complete with arched halls, armament, and shields.

The decor emphasizes the building's structure. Oak beams, that appear in ceilings throughout the building, the exposed stone of the walls, and the raw details of the forged metal all seem softened by letting in sunlight and by using gentle fabrics such as the endearing petit point.

All the delights of Normandy, the land of William the Conqueror, such as its meadows, apple trees, and coast between Arromanches and Courseulles, all serve as the basis of the cuisine on the tables of La Rençonnière. One of the best reasons for visiting this hotel is to experience the regional cuisine.

Another great reason is that la Ferme specializes in providing a restful place for personal rejuvenation, a place for study and comtemplation in total peace. The scenery invites this and the hotel service ensures it.

The hotel is located in an
old fortification.

View and detail of the dining room
with stone walls, dominated by a
large fireplace.

An austere decor with a profusion of
fabrics embroidered in petit point
predominates in the rooms.

The wooden beams reinforce the elegant, rustic style of this double room. Next to the beds,
a desk with a lamp fills the corner of the room. The rug enhances the area.

Villa San Michele

Fiesole, Florence, Italy

The idyllic region of Tuscany surrounds this impressive fifteenth-century Franciscan monastery which has been transformed into a wonderfully enchanting hotel. The hotel is only 16 miles from Florence in the small town of Fiesole.

The Villa de San Michele owes its name to the archangel Michael and its facade is attributed to Michelangelo. Founded as a monastery in the fifteenth century by the Romiti Terzari of Saint Francis, it was subsequently renovated by Giovanni Bartolomeo Davanzati.

The original Renaissance style was transformed with the passing of the centuries into that of an elegant bourgeois villa. The building was seriously damaged during the Second World War by bombs. In 1950, Monsieur Lucien Teissier acquired it and began a radical restoration with the help of architect Emilio Terry and of the Florentine authorities. They have transformed it while preserving the purity of the Renaissance style and ensuring that the interior design reflected the ambiance of the sixteenth and seventeenth centuries.

The hotel has 26 rooms available. These were monks' cells in former times, and guests may savor their atmosphere of utmost serenity. From the side portico, which dates from the year 1600, or from the pool, one finds exceptional views of Florence and of the hills on the opposite bank of the Arno. From the rear garden, guests may enjoy views of the dense grove of trees, which include oaks, Tuscan cypresses, and olive trees. Two ancient stone chapels also stand nearby. The floors of the hotel, covered soberly in brick, the interior walls decorated in pale yellow with small ornamentations, and the patios with their true classical peristyles, all call to mind the timeless peace of the monastery. In the dining hall and in the sitting rooms, guests may enjoy the same peace, made even richer by the sound of piano music and by one of the finest collections of antique furniture in Italy. In the ancient Loggia, an open-air restaurant with views of Florence offers Tuscan delicacies such as petti fagianella farciti alla castagna or filetto di cinghiale.

In the garden of the old monastery, guests may enjoy the extraordinary enchantment of the Tuscan sunlight. Olive trees, cypresses, oaks, and springtime flowers surround Villa San Michele.

View of the reception area of the hotel, with a lamp and a small altar in the background.

Panoramic view of the Loggia Restaurant. Some hallways of the monastery have been converted into enclosed terraces. Roller blinds have been installed to soften the light.

View of Florence from the side portico of the hotel.

The Cenacolo Bar. A fresco of the Last Supper looms over the space, whose ambiance is defined by Persian rugs and antique furnishings.

Villa San Michele **69**

château tour des puits

Savoy, France

The Tour des Puits Château is located between the park at Bauges, which is a sanctuary of pristine natural beauty, and the Belledonne Chain, in the middle of Savoy near the historic Lyon route to Turin. The château is surrounded by seven hectares of lush parks and gardens, and has an nearly rectangular plan, slate roofing, and a stylized tower. It was decorated and renovated by Jean Michel Villot, Olivier Caion, and Christophe Polewski of JMV, with effects reminiscent of former inhabitants such as Baroness Marie Antoinette du Bettonet or Sir Pierre de Puits. This lovely example of the architecture of the rural French nobility now has seven exclusive rooms only.

The decoration of the establishment is a synthesis of classical styles and rustic elegance, with bedrooms that have been finished off with baldachins, parquets with finished antiques, marbles, rugs, and furniture in traditional style. The hotel, which belongs to the Relais & Châteaux chain, also has at its disposal a pool, which is set alongside the rich greenery of the gardens, and a fine restaurant where one may savor the specialties of Savoyard cuisine, such as filet de Lavaret from the lakes of Savoy or the cheeses of the region. Its excellent location allows guests to enjoy picturesque hikes and excursions in the surrounding region, either on bicycle or in a calash. Likewise, one may wish to discover the historic routes such as the circuit of the dukes of Savoy.

Detail of the pool area with pool house.

The hotel dining room has large windows that look out onto the garden.

Nighttime view of the main facade of Château Tour des Puits .

Bedroom with a baldachin and classical furnishings with a romantic inspiration.

Rugs and period pieces help all the bedrooms achieve a refined appearance.

the point

Saranac Lake, NY, USA

The Point is considered one of the top hotels in the United States. It was an old property of the Rockefeller family, and was the home of William Avery Rockefeller. In a wooded ten-acre strip of land between Lake Saranac and the Upper Saranac, a set of buildings was constructed for receiving occasional visitors and for providing them with tranquility, convenience, and time amidst the pristine forest for enjoying the Adirondacks and the serene waters of Lake Serenac.

The Point upholds this tradition, maintaining the buildings and the configuration of the original spaces. Even the decoration follows the same guidelines, for the simple reason that they are the most suitable. They include elements such as the generous use of woods, broad furniture for sitting and resting, the fabrics in warm and dark tones contrasting with the pointed subtlety of the tulles, the soft rugs accentuating the inviting character of the original wood floor, and a worthwhile antique that bringing out the personality of a corner of a room. All this is helpful in maintaining the welcoming and sumptuous tone and the greatest degree of comfort in the Adirondack Mountains.

Set among the trees, this charming hotel has 11 rooms in four separate buildings. All rooms have a view of the lake and a private bathroom that is remarkably spacious. The bathrooms have bronze overlays on an original design and chrome accessories. Each room features a different combination of local regional furniture, antiques, rugs, and wood in the floor and frequently in the ceiling as well. Furthermore, each room has a sculpted stone hearth. The entire hotel complex has been designed with leisure in mind: gentle activities such as sports and taking walks.

View of the wharf with one of the rooms in the upper part.

The main lodge, which includes the Algonquin, Iroquois, Morningside, and Mohawk rooms, takes on the appearance of being a typical mountain cabin during winter.

View of the lake region with an impressive sunset. In the background is the wharf.

From their rooms, guests have exceptional views over Lake Serenac.

The hotel has all the equipment necessary for fishing available.

The boathouse, an enormous structure built out over the water, also has personality. The boats are moored below the boathouse when not in use.

On the second floor, a large terrace surrounds the entire building. Each room has an area for food, a bar, and a large bed with a canopy. Outdoors, guests may enjoy picnic areas, trails between the woods, and small coves where they may bask in the sun on the shores of the lake.

The region has always been a fisherman's paradise, and The Point offers its guests all the equipment they might need for fishing: poles and tackle, as well as canoes, rowboats, and sailboats.

The Great Salon has been specially decorated for the Christmas holidays.

Guests at The Point enjoy a meal of refined cuisine in an atmosphere made more intimate by candles and a warm fireplace.

The Mohawk room is a favorite of the guests because of its height, its decoration, and its magnificent views of the lake.

The Iroquois room is located in the Main Lodge. It has decor originally chosen by the daughter of William Rockefeller.

Evensong was the private bedroom of the Rockefellers in their final years. It is decorated with white pine wood and has a stone fireplace.

An exceptional room in the converted wharf has a canopied bed with white and green tulles.

Morningside, with its walls and ceilings covered with white pine and a large fireplace around which armchairs have been placed.

Saignon Hotel

Saignon, France

In the heart of a place north of Luberon, called Saignon, there is a hotel that accommodates artists who are working under the auspices of an art association. The hotel accommodates only up to eight people. The hotel is also open to the general public all year long. Saignon is located on the legendary plateau of the Claparèdes at an altitude of 480 meters, and overlooks the valley of Calavon.

The hotel building itself is large and rather expensive to maintain, but the owners preferred not to convert it into a conventional hotel. They opted instead for comfort and simplicity. The bedspreads are new, and the wood and metal furniture is traditional and simple. The walls are painted in ocre and rust colors, with each room painted in a different color. The floors are tiled in the traditional Provençal style. The bathrooms, painted blue, have been remodeled in a way that preserves the old fixtures. The owners also opted for a casual decor that respected the building's history.

All the rooms have contemporary art, and some have frescos painted by artists such as the Belgian Koen Theys.

The principle that guides the activity of the hotel-residence is rooted in a lifestyle or attitude toward the plastic arts as a part of daily life and therefore the artists to work in a rural setting during the most pleasant seasons of the year. During these same seasons the owners are also enticed to combine truffles and other foods and flavors with the visual, tactile, and olfactory pleasures of the region.

The lower floor of the hotel has the dining room, the kitchen (where delicious breakfasts and lunches are shared among the artists and guests), a salon-gallery, and various rooms dedicated to office duties. A reading room is on the second floor next to three of the bedrooms, separated by a wide hallway that leads to the bathrooms. The third floor is devoted to the art studios. These are not only for resident artists, but also for the other guests to practice and experiment in. The studios are large. Three are inside and one is outside. The outside studio is for use by artists who work with heavy materials. The hotel

Main facade of the hotel.

Several sculptures are on exposition on the bare stone patios.

Detail of a small shutter. The loop curtains add a touch of romance.

The hotel has long, narrow hallways that are reminiscent of old country homes.

Main salon.

also has a charming garden, which is accessible through a passageway. The entire hotel has central heating and also fireplaces, which add to the hotel's ambiance. As a result of new telecommunications technologies, the hotel is experimenting with creating a kind of virtual academy in collaboration with artists and universities.

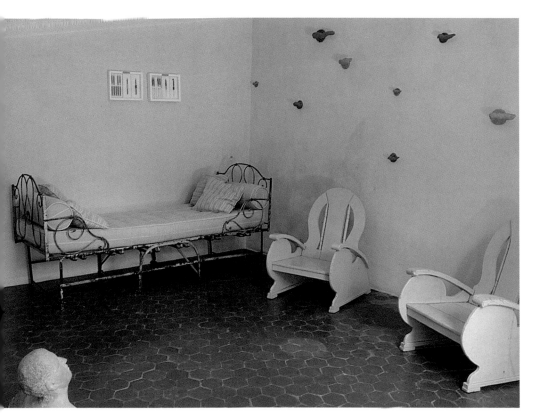

Detail of the hallway.

All of the rooms in the hotel have designer furniture.

The eating area has a cozy atmosphere. The furniture is from antique brokerages.

A fireplace presides over this
room.

Detail of the garden.

Bathroom with a pedestal bathtub.

The hotel has numerous works of
contemporary art.

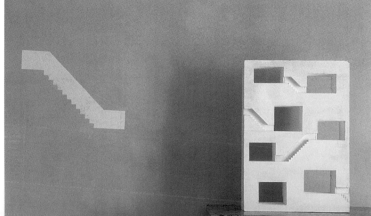

Bedroom area. The color combinations of strawberry and kiwi green contrast with the muted tones of the painting on the walls.

Old wooden doors separate the various areas of the bedroom.

The rooms have minimalist decor that bring to mind a Mediterranean atmosphere.

CHEWTON GLEN HOTEL

Hampshire, UK

This peaceful, 70-acre estate, 90 miles from London, presides over the forests and gardens of Hampshire. From the building's proportions, it is clear that this is a Georgian-style mansion that dates from the beginning of the eighteenth century, but which has undergone various renovations and expansions. At the beginning of the twentieth century, Colonel Edward Tinker, who was at that time the owner, had the facade rebuilt with brick.

The Skan family acquired the hotel in 1996 and undertook a meticulous plan to modernize it. This program is ongoing. Presently, the hotel has 33 rooms and 19 suites, each of which is decorated differently in an elegant, rustic style in which fabrics and wood predominate.

The hotel offers a gymnasium with facial massage and beauty treatments available, as well as a covered, Romantic-style swimming pool, weight-training rooms, and covered tennis courts. Also available is a beautiful outdoor heated pool, a nine-hole golf course, a croquet course, and hiking trails that allow guests to experience the enchantment of old England. The Marryat restaurant, recipient of numerous awards, offers an opportunity to get to know first hand the best cuisine of the region as created by Chef Pierre Chevillard, with an eclectic culinary style based on fresh local foods such as mushrooms and quarry from New Forest.

The Chewton Glen has been honored throughout its history. In 1998 it was voted by the Condé Nast Traveler magazine's Gold List as the top hotel in Europe and thirteenth worldwide. It has also been chosen by the Booker Prize of Excellence as the best hotel, and by Condé Nast Traveler Readers Choice Award as the best holiday hotel in the United Kingdom.

Chewton Glen Hotel **85**

An attractive terrace surrounded
by flowers and trees has been
added next to the garden.

The outdoor pool frames the
rear area of the hotel.

A glassed-in terrace provides a spacious, cheerfully lit dining area where guests can savor Chef Pierre Chevillard's dishes.

Detail of one of the rooms defined by a profusion of flowery drapes, one of the hallmarks of English interior design.

Detail of one of the salons characterized by period paintings and classic furnishings.

The Chewton Glen offers its guests private nooks, which are austerely and elegantly decorated.

View of an exterior corner of the hotel.

The large indoor pool creates a romantic English atmosphere. The space framed by massive columns refers to the proportions of classical architecture.

Interior salons with elegant, classical decor

From the vantage point of their rooms, guests may admire the lovely gardens surrounding the establishment.

HOSTALET 1701

Regencós, Girona, Spain

The couple who have owned and managed this enchanting hotel since its inauguration in April, 1998, use the phrase "Open year round" to sum up their concept of the hotel. The hotel is nestled in the heart of a region that is without a doubt blessed with a gentle climate all year. In winter, guests may take excursions to the small nearby towns or play golf on the gorgeous plain of Ampurdan, which lies only five minutes from the hotel. Of course, guests may also delight themselves with the wonderful gastronomy of the region. The fact that the hotel is only an hour's drive by car from the cities of Barcelona or Gerona also allows guests to partake of more cosmopolitan experiences if the wish.

In summer the hotel's charm is even more obvious. Hostalet 1701 is located in the small town of Regencós, five minutes from the Costa Brava, where one may find the most attractive beaches in this part of the Mediterranean. Sun, tranquillity, shopping, leisure, sports, and exciting nightlife are all conveniently available nearby. The hotel also offers mountain bike and Zodiac boat rentals.

The hotel was built in the town's main square at the beginning of the eighteenth century, originally as what is called in Catalonia a *masia pairal*, a type of family dwelling intended to house up to three generations.

The reception area of the hotel is on the lower floor, and has a beautiful set with a table, chair, and lamp that have all been recovered from an old house in the region. The lower floor also has a room for showing and selling antiques and a well-equipped kitchen with a rustic atmosphere. The kitchen offers a light breakfast based on the typical local bread-with-tomato dish, as well as locally made sausages, eggs, croissants, toast with preserves, juices, coffee, and milk. No restaurant service is provided, although guests may order lunches or dinners in advance if they wish.

The three guest rooms are on the second floor. These rooms have a cozy atmosphere and have been individually decorated. All three have a

full bath. The furniture in the rooms is all for sale, as is the furniture in the entire hotel.

Part of the roof has been fitted out as a balcony with a hammock for reading, relaxing, or for enjoying the magnificent views. This area may soon be converted into a fourth guest room, however.

The owners have paid utmost attention to detail in order to provide guests with an environment of absolute quiet and total independence, even to the point that the owners are present only during certain times of day. Guests have access to the main door so that they may come and go as they wish.

The porch at the entrance to the hotel still accommodates the town's only mailbox.

The entire lower floor has access to the outside. This door provides separate access to the antique shop.

The kitchen. Here guests may enjoy one other's company over lunch.

A few sculptures are on display on the bare stone patios.

Details at reception

The antique shop is also on the lower floor.

The second floor, where the rooms
are located, has a double level that
is accessible by means of stairs.
The stairs also lead to the upper
porch of the hotel.

A sitting room outside
the guest room area
provides space for
reading and relaxing.

The furnishings in the guest rooms have been gathered from local farm houses, and all are for sale.

Each of the three rooms has been individually decorated, as have the bathrooms.

This small work area enjoys abundant lighting because of the window.

Guest room number two has painted wooden headboards, a ceiling with wooden beams, and an enchanting bathroom.

The highest space in the hotel is currently being use as an area for lounging, reading, and comtemplation, but it may soon be made into a fourth guest room.

réaux Hotel

Bourgueil, France

The Château de Réaux is located in the heart of the region of the Loire, in what is known as the Valley of the Kings. This area is near Orleans and is well known for its Chinon and Bourgueil wines. Castles and palaces are scattered throughout the region due to the fact that it had been the royal residence before the monarchs finally established themselves in Paris.

Built in the fifteenth century, the Château de Réaux can be made out from a distance by its entrance pavilion flanked by two towers decorated with stone and checkerboard brick. The château has belonged to the present owners for more than a century, and today the hotel is recognized for its exquisite decor and gastronomy. Réaux is located in the center of a beautiful wooded setting on the banks of the Loire River, and from here guests may enjoy going out for boat rides or hiking, horseback riding, or golfing.

The hotel has tennis courts available, and offers 17 rooms and 4 suites, all of which have been marvelously decorated in distinct styles, such as Barois with Oriental motifs. Many of the rooms offer direct access to the garden. An annex, called the cottage, also exists, and it houses six additional rooms for the guests.

The moat that surrounds the château, the meticulously maintained garden, and the perfectly preserved historical architecture all serve to define the atmosphere of the hotel. Regardless of the vantage point, the eye is met by an idyllic panorama. Through the restaurant windows, for example, one sees a countryside whose charm reflects its centuries of cultivation. In contrast to the sober sitting rooms, with their crafted wood, Persian rugs, and period furniture, a combination of yellows and blues lends a youthful Mediterranean feel to the interior of the restaurant.

Exposed stone and Gothic windows decorate the outer rooms of the hotel.

Sitting room in which one immediately notices the rugs, teardrop lamps, the antique stone chimney, and the fire-red tone of the walls.

Detail of the furnishing.

The Persian rugs frame a piece of period furniture covered in brilliant materials. The silver service stands out on the small auxiliary table.

An imposing Oriental-style canopy is the centerpiece of this room done in Romantic style.

View of the restaurant with its elegant table service.

Bedroom with Mediterranean flavor in which blues and the wooden beams play a major role.

Château Roumégouse

Gramat, Le Quercy, France

The Hotel de la Roumégouse is located in the northern portion of the department of Lot, in an area known as Le Quercy, a natural extension of the Dordogne Valley. This region is richly dotted with medieval villages. The hotel is part of the Relais & Châteaux chain, and is located in a château that was totally rebuilt in a Neogothic Renaissance style during the nineteenth century. The château is surrounded by an exceptionally beautiful, hundred-year-old, five-hectare park that includes a ziggurat, or tower of Babel, which offers extraordinary views of Rocamadour and its surroundings. The château was acquired thirty years ago by its present owners, Luce and Jean Louis Lainé, who then transformed it. Luce now takes charge of the interior decoration and Jean Louis takes charge of the kitchen. Although the structures have been maintained since the remodeling, each year the decor of the salons and rooms are changed. The rooms are characterized by a classical style whose tone is set by well-chosen antiques, including several Napoleon III, Louis XIII, and Louis XV pieces.

Roumégouse Château has fifteen bedrooms, two of which have been converted into comfortable apartments. All of the rooms have been decorated in a unique way with antique furniture, Turkish rugs, French and Spanish fabrics, wallpaper, crafted wooden headrests, seventeenth- and eighteenth-century beds, and small bouquets created by the proprietor herself with flowers from the surrounding grounds.

The hotel has a small library that features prominent wood paneling and a salon with Napoleon III furniture, including upholstery and robust carpets in burgundy tones. There are three dining rooms: one in Louis XIII style, another in Louis XV style, and one which is a terrace with a gallery framed by hundreds of white geraniums. From this terrace, guests may admire the Rocamadour plateau, which can be glimpsed behind the hedged-in pool, while at the same time they may enjoy the internationally recognized cooking of the Perigord, such as its foies and truffles.

Aerial view of Roumégouse Château showing its rectangular layout, typical of Neogothic structures which are often crowned by circular towers. Also clearly seen is the pool surrounded by hedges and a lush stand of mature trees.

A large, wooden panel frames an entire semicircular wall which features fabrics with historical motifs. Defining the ambience is bar furniture and two-person sofas with rough upholstery.

This Louis XIII dining room achieves a gracious, medieval atmosphere thanks to the combination of the apricot tone of the walls, the dark woods, and the prominence of a large stone chimney with pewter objects.

Main salon decorated with Napoleon III furniture. The burgundy tones contrast with the wooden beams and the floral decor. The dog of the house relaxes on the rug.

Another of the dining rooms of Roumégouse Château. This one is in Louis XV brought up to date with floral design and salmon-tone fabrics.

Master bedroom with an attic ceiling. In order to further emphasize the inclination of the ceiling, the walls have been painted a pastel yellow and the bed has been done in neutral colors.

Overall view of a bedroom suite showing a king-size bed decked out with a pleated curtain at the headboard. A small rest area with a sofa and nineteenth century writing desk complete the decor.

château plessis

Plessis, Mayenne, France

This castle is located near a river in leafy forests, and opens to the visitor its charming history along with the customs and special way of life of those who have lived here. After negotiating the twists and turns of the narrow roads that wind through the heart of this region near the Loire known as Mayenne, the visitor comes to a hedge that hides a long corridor of well-manicured grass at the end of which lies the Château de Plessis. Once the visitor sets foot on the 40 hectares of woods and gardens that surround the château, he or she realizes that this is a place where one could learn to savor the pleasure of life.

The château was built as a country home for nobility. The greenhouse and the kitchen date from the sixteenth century and the rest of the château dates from the eighteenth. The exact date of construction is now unknown because the parish that held the records for the property was destroyed during the French Revolution.

Paul and Simone Benoist, the present owners of the hotel, continue the property's tradition as being a family residence. Initially, they planned to live a quiet life there alone, but some American friends who were spending the summer in Plessis persuaded them to open the château to guests who wished to experience the French country lifestyle in an intimate way.

The main part of the château has three floors. The first floor has a salon, a main hall, dining room, and kitchen. The salon itself is divided into two spaces. The chairs and the chest of drawers in the salon are Louis XV, the mahogony bureau is Spanish. The paintings are by Boucher and date from the eighteenth century. The dining room is painted light blue and has a decorative border showing carriage races. The Louis XV chairs in the dining room are works of art. Most of the silver is Christofle.

A large wooden table flanked by two benches of equal size separate the kitchen, which has fired clay tiling. An interesting detail is the walnut wood lining in the freezer. (Simone organizes marvelous dinners for her guests.)

A broad staircase leads to the upper floors where the eight guest rooms

of the château are located. Each of the rooms has its own bathroom and its own style of decor, including such decorative elements as exposed beams, built-in wardrobes, and Louis XV books.

Paul and Simone want to receive their guests as friends, sharing meals and having coffee together in the garden, for example, but at the same time they want to allow their guests complete independence.

The hotel organizes enchanting tours in hot air balloons so that guests may enjoy spectacular views of the countryside.

Night view of the hotel.

The rear facade of the château also has charm.

The main salon includes a separate space that serves as a sitting room.

The guest rooms are located in upper floors of the château. The clock dates from the nineteenth century.

Detail of the salon, showing how the garden is directly accessible.

Most of the silver is Christofle, making these true
works of art.

One of the bathrooms, with an attic ceiling. Before the renovation, the château had only
one bathroom and lacked central heating.

The decor in each room has been personalized. Shown here is the "bird room." The marble
fireplace is on the central axis of the room.

Detail of the dining room. The chairs are Louis XVI.

Detail of the sitting area in one of the rooms. This room is blue with paintings hanging on all the walls.

Les terrasses

Ibiza, Spain

This lovely hotel is located on the highway that ties Santa Eulàlia with the city of Ibiza on the Spanish Balearic island that is also named Ibiza. The entrance from the main highway is rather hard to find, as it is identifiable only by an enormous blue stone that has been placed at the head of the dirt road leading to the hotel. The hotel itself has as its nucleus a country house that is typical of the region. Previously in ruins, the farm retains all its charm, with broad white walls that protect from the sun and that have been built in a rather anarchical manner around the various terraces in a way that is typical example of Ibizan charm.

Surrounding the house is the kitchen, dining room, sitting room, and the office and living quarters of the director and proprietor of the hotel, who has personally taken care to imbue each of the rooms with a special charm by giving them a distinct and suitable decor. The pool and the gardens cover the surroundings of the hotel up to the area where the rooms are, in the highest part of the terrain. All the guest quarters are divided into three comfortable environments; namely, a living area, a bedroom, and a bathroom. All differ from each other and all have been decorated with a sense of wit and humor. Throughout the rooms antique furnishings have been used, many of these coming from flea markets held on weekends in local towns. The main suite includes a large living room, bedroom, complete bath, terrace, and a delightful covered porch with its own shower and basin. The rooms of the entire hotel are whitewashed. The doors and windows are framed in an indigo blue. All the colors have been extracted from genuine natural pigments that are found in plants growing on the island.

The effect achieved corresponds more to that of a vacation home than to a hotel.

*The main patio opens onto the lounge-dining room.
During the winter months, a screen can be unfolded
to offer protection against the cold.*

*Upper photograph: The facades of the hotel make use of indigo,
the emblematic color of the island.
Lower photograph: View of the summer dining room.*

The pool faces the entrance. Several lounge chairs and a table for lunches and breakfasts have been placed around the pool. A yellow glass cover for the pool gives the water a Nile-green appearance. The hotel also has a small swimming pool surrounded by vegetation, with a hammock where guests may relax after dinner.

The bedroom and sitting room of the suite with a king-size bed and two sofas. The rest of the furniture has come from open-air flea markets held on weekends in nearby towns.

The bathroom of the suite. The wall has been dressed in marble.

One of the bathrooms of the hotel.
The hotel director designed the
counter top.

A curtain protects the area around
the shower in the suite. The bed has a
wooden base.

One of the nine rooms for guests.
Besides having one of the beds on
the floor, the bath is integrated
into the room itself.

The shower in this room is
hidden behind a
handcrafted curtain.

The fabric of the padding of the shower curtain adds color to the room.
The wooden furnishings are restorations.

Hacienda Katanchel

Merida, Yucatan, Mexico

Built in the jungle a half-hour's drive from the coast of Mexico's Yucatan Peninsula, Hacienda Katanchel embodies the exoticism of an old Spanish encomienda. In the Mayan language, katanchel means "where people consult the bow in the sky." Years ago, the remains of a large platform with five pyramidal structures were discovered 16 miles from the city of Merida by architect Aníbal González and archeologist/botanist Mónica Hernández. These structures may have been a Mayan astronomical observatory.

The property that Aníbal and Mónica have restored illustrates the splendor of Neo-Hispanic architecture as well as the mystery of the Mayan civilization that preceded it. For more than thirty years after its discovery, it lay abandoned and overgrown by jungle, with trees growing up to the rooftops. The haciendas of the Yucatan came from the encomiendas, or lands that the Spanish Crown granted to the soldiers of the Conquista. The haciendas symbolize the genesis of a civilization that emerged from the blending of Mayan and Spanish cultures.

During the nineteenth century, the Yucatan region experienced a glorious period at the peak of world demand for hemp, which was used to make rope. As a result, the owners of the haciendas became extremely wealthy and the sober buildings were remodeled and enlarged until they became palaces. This boom ended with the invention of nylon.

Today, the Katanchel Hacienda is one of the most charming hotels in the world. Its owners organize exploratory tours to visit towns lost in the jungle and experience their typical fiestas and original artisanry, romantic mineral water springs, exotic restaurants, and abandoned monasteries.

The hacienda has 40 rooms with a private pool. The hacienda's restaurant, Casa de Máquinas, has been recognized by a New York trade magazine as one of Mexico's five best.

The establishment is surrounded by orchards and gardens where vegetables are grown organically.

The hotel guests can swim in old irrigation tanks that have been converted into small pools.

Gardens and lush vegetation surround this pool that has been built of teak wood.

The interior has Spanish Colonial decor.

Main suite with private pool.

Large fans make air
conditioning unnecessary in
the dining room, where the
vividly contrasting colors are a
part of the decor.

Detail of one of the salons.

The game room has a pool table.

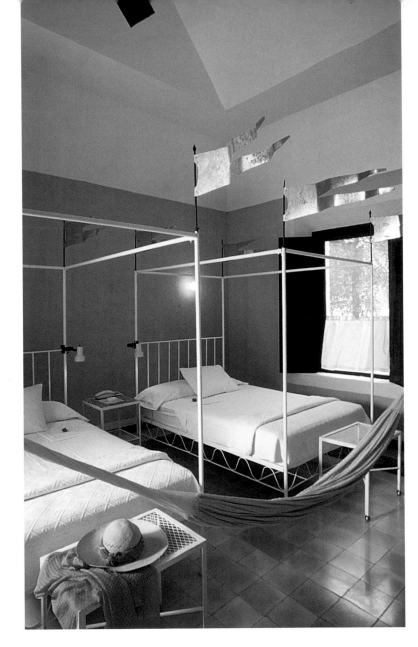

The rooms have a minimalist decor that is reminiscent of Mediterranean tastes.

Hacienda Benazuza

Sanlúcar la Mayor, Sevilla, Spain

One of the most charming hotels in Andulusia is a hotel called Hacienda Benazuza in Sanlúcar la Mayor, in the heart of the Comarca del Aljarafe near the Guadiamar River. Only 15 minutes from Seville, the hotel is built in a tenth century alquería, or farmhouse. It is a small oasis surrounded by hundred-year-old olive trees. The hotel has been remodeled and transformed into a modern establishment by Manolo Gaviria and his team.

Seen from a distance, the most outstanding aspect of the building is the complicated combination of roofs that spread out at various heights, sustained by large stretches of wall that stand out thanks to a blend of ocher, whitewash, and vivid yellow. Inside the hotel all the rooms have been organized around the patios. The design of the interior is one that enhances a sense of restfulness through the notable use of spaces cast in an almost sultry shadow, and where the gardens with their murmuring fountains evoke Arab concepts of interior design.

Hacienda Benazuza has available 26 rooms and 18 suites decorated with antique furniture of Spanish and English origin, stuccoed walls, and magnificent art objects. The Arab-Andalusian gardens, with fountains and waterfalls, are interspersed with palms. Surrounding the hotel is a French garden and a wooded area with more than forty species.

The three restaurants, La Alquería, El Patio, and La Alberca, offer specialties of both international and Andalusian cuisine, and the bar El Guadarnes offers an ample assortment of cocktails.

At sundown, the light brings out the sienna ocher of the walls and the old alquería, and the water reflects the Arab-Andalusian vegetation of Benazuza.

An antique well dotted with plants is the centerpiece of this space.

Sets of color and lines: the pungent yellow defines the walls, while the roofs of various heights finish off the look of the hotel.

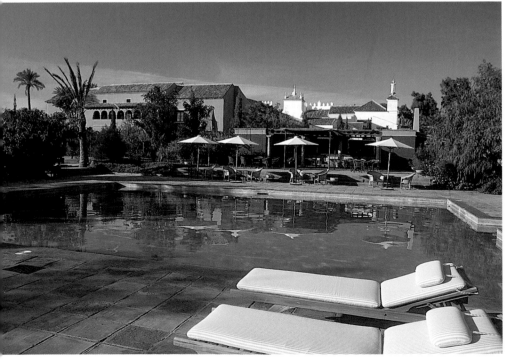

The simplicity of the architecture allows guests to enjoy the atmosphere or an old Andalusian hacienda.

View of the outdoor pool, showing the teak furnishings dressed out with sailcloth.

View of the countryside surrounding Seville, as seen from one of the restaurants.

Bedroom with sumptuous antique beds that contrast with the stucco walls.

Indoor patio with sienna ocher, dominated by arches and columns.

The rooms have preserved a rural flavor of the old Andalusian country estates.

In the Hacienda Benazuza one may savor international and Andalusian cuisines in an atmosphere of rustic elegance.

Recreation area. Detail of the billiards room.

Detail of one of the bathrooms. The Neapolitan marble bathtub has been finished off with semicircular curtains.

Under the ceiling with wooden beams, a king-size bed with pleated curtains is the centerpiece of a suite that is distinguished by its harmonious use of warm colors such as yellow and apricot. At the foot of the bed is a covered footrest.

el castell

La Seu d'Urgell, Lleida, Spain

El Castell is an extraordinary hotel opened in 1973 under the
management of the Tapies family. The hotel is built on the remains
of an historical fortification called Castellciutat, which played an
important role in defending the frontier with France by controlling
an Andorran Pyrenees mountain pass that lies directly in front of
the hotel. The present structure uses the fortress as an architectural
background. This fortress-watchtower perched upon a rocky
Pyrenees massif served as a departure point for Jaume Tapies in
1973. He began with this immense stone fortress, whose military
past contrasted sharply with the surrounding idyllic green meadows
of the Urgellet. He then labored to complete a hotel that is
characterized by its ample spaces and its exceptional views, its
generous use of wood contrasting with original stone, by the high
quality of its services, and by its excellent restaurant.

The thirty-seven rooms of the hotel are all decorated in a unique and
personal way. Guests may choose between attic spaces with ceilings
lined with pine wood or suites with a private garden. All rooms have
views of the Cadí-Moixeró nature park. The furnishings are massive,
and are made with cherry or walnut in the guest rooms and with
pine in the attic spaces. The bathrooms have either Portuguese
marble or travertine. The guest rooms and the common spaces all
have wide windows and a restful atmosphere. The constant
remodeling and redecorating has over the years turned El Castell
into a charming and cozy establishment.

The Castell has made its restaurant a point of pride, and the restaurant
has received a star in the Michelin Guide. Dishes such as quail
thighs stuffed with truffle, or potato terrine with lobster and a
zabaglione of caviar have become classics at the restaurant, in
addition to dishes based on the high-quality local vegetables and
lamb. The dining room is impressive, with its large stone arcades, its
tapestries, the heavy wood of its furnishings, and its broad windows.
With its rugged grandeur, the dining room demonstrates the
pleasant synthesis between the architecture of El Castell and its
excellent restaurant.

Interior of the dining room
with its remarkable arcades.

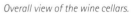

Lower photographs:
A fireplace is the centerpiece of
this room.

Overall view of the wine cellars.

The guest rooms exude a
certain Mediterranean sense.

Hotels by the Sea

Las brisas Hotel

San José, Ibiza, Spain

The hotel is located on Porroig Point, at the edge of a cliff that overlooks the bay of Es Cubells. Five minutes away on foot, an unspoiled cove shelters a beach that is bordered by pines, where one may have lunch in a comfortable eatery while running one's feet through the sand. The city of Ibiza, which is known for its ambiance and its unforgettable parties, is fifteen minutes away by car.

The hotel owes its distinctive personality to a few surprising and lively colors as well to its Mediterranean decor. An atmosphere of tranquility prevails in the hotel, as a result of the placement of several sitting rooms next to a garden patio and also because of a few Oriental touches.

In the evening, guests may have a drink at the bar near the pool and watch the sunset. The hotel consists of three suites and six rooms, all of which have a private terrace and a view of the sea. Each is decorated in a different style, and great care has clearly been taken with details. The rooms are equipped with air conditioning, satellite TV, telephone, minibar, and a safe. The two so-called Junior Suites, set on the second floor, have a 50-square-meter terrace with a pergola that shades a comfortable sitting room. The VIP suite is divided into a living room, bedroom (with a stereo and fax), and a 150-square-meter shaded terrace. The hotel also has a tennis court and a bicycle track for use by the guests. If the guests wish to rent a car or boat, Emmanuel and René will recommend the most suitable solution, and will point out the most beautiful places on the island.

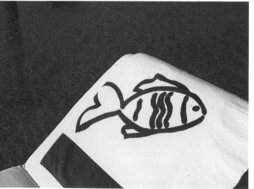

Detail showing an example of purely Mediterranean-style decor.

The hotel captures the genuine architectural style of the island of Ibiza.

Las Brisas is built upon an imposing cliff, from which spectacular sunsets can be enjoyed.

On the following page, the large photograph at the bottom: detail of one of the sitting rooms characterized by Mediterranean decor with a few Oriental touches.

The natural fiber roof allows light to pass, creating beautiful effects on the openwork walls.

Rugged furniture of forged metal with rough fabrics are on the terraces.

Arcades connect the inside with the lovely gardens.

On the following page:
a baldachin finished off
with curtains frames an old
metal bed in one of the
suites of the hotel.

The tiling is the center of
attention in this
bathroom illuminated by
natural light.

The clay floors and the
ornamental painting
add warmth to the
corners near the
windows of the room.

GUANAHANI HOTEL

Saint Barthélemy, French Antilles

The Guanahani, a small hotel for vacationers on the island of Saint
Barthélemy, runs from the tops of the hills of Grand Cul de Sac,
gently embracing the entire bay. Discovered by Christopher
Columbus, Saint Barthélemy is an island of volcanic origin that is
located 230 kilometers from Guadaloupe, and is bathed by the
Atlantic on the east and the Caribbean on the west.
The tremendously clear waters surrounding it are an intense blue,
with coral reefs nearby. The entire island is dazzlingly colorful: the
deep greens of the vegetation, the intense blues and turquoises of
the sea and the horizon, the basaltic black of the volcanic rocks, the
whites splashed with pinks and reds of the tropical and
Mediterranean vegetation brought by the European colonists.
Tamarinds, palms, coconuts, white and pink laurels, and an endless
variety of species of birds, such as the brown pelican, hummingbird,
or blackbird, make Saint Barthélemy a unique paradise.
The hotel, which belongs to the chain called the Leading Hotels of the
World, sprawls over six hectares of magnificent tropical gardens,
and combines a style that is unequivocally Caribbean with
European comfort.
The hotel reception can be glimpsed all along the serpentine line of
bougainvilleas. The reception area brings to mind the homes from
the colonial period. The Guanahani has available 76 rooms, 18 of
which have recently been remodeled and 13 of which are suites that
include private pools. The rooms are arranged as bungalows
scattered between tropical park and the ocean. The architects and
interior designers have considered every last detail: the furnishings
and accessories are done in natural materials such as white cedar
wood and turquoise, while much of the furniture is wicker and the
fabrics used are cotton. The ceiling fans inevitably suggest the
colonial age, although in fact the hotel of course has central air
conditioning. The baths in the rooms are done in a unbridled modern
design and feature marble as a central element.
The kitchen in the Guanahani is also extraordinary. In the indoor
restaurant Bartolomeo, one may dine from a varied Mediterranean
menu. On the porch next to the pool is the unmistakably Caribbean
space known as the Indigo, where guests may enjoy unrivaled views
in the open air.

A private pool that is
part of a suite.

Guests may relax in the open air of a tropical garden at the hotel restaurant Indigo.

Detail of the hotel decor where
pastel colors such as green and
rosewood are combined.

The interior of the hotel shows a
colonial style brought up to date
with modern wall papers and
chromatic contrasts in the walls.

One of the rooms where cedar wood and turquoise tones play a strong role in the design.

jake's place

Treasure Beach, Jamaica

View of the building's extexrior.

One of the beaches at the hotel. Detail of a small wooden shutter.

View of one of the bedrooms with a typically Arabic or Mediterranean pointed arch.

Jake's is decorated in an eclectic style with Greek, Mexican, and Jamaican strokes.

Overall view of one of the bedrooms.

Jake's Place is a group of eight pastel-colored cabins found in one of the most charming little bays of the Caribbean. Located in the small fishing community of Treasure Beach on Jamaica's peaceful southern coast, the hotel is a two-hour drive from the airport at Montego Bay and a half hour from Negril. The family-owned establishment opened its doors in 1995. Sally Henzell designed the hotel's interior. The decoration of the rooms presents an eclectic mixture of styles that have been skillfully blended. The blend includes Jamaican influences, of course, but also Greek, Mexican, and even a strain of Catalan Modernism, considering the owners' passion for the work of Gaudí.

All of the rooms are only a few steps from the sea, where guests may enjoy diving, fishing, rowing, or simply sunbathing on the private beach or in the salt water pool. Guests may also enjoy guided tours, visiting such places as a waterfall or a deserted island, or they may take a river safari.

Each room is decorated with Jamaican antiques and local art. The rooms do not have telephones, televisions, or even air conditioning (instead, they rely on sea breezes and ceiling fans).

Dining at the hotel restaurant, guests may choose from among the finest specialties of Jamaican cuisine. After an excellent meal they may walk to the straw-roof dance halls.

A new area, called the "Seapuss," has recently been opened at Jake's. In keeping with the overall philosophy of the hotel, a store called the "Casla Tree" has been opened in a simple cabin where, among other things, typical Jamaican crafts may be purchased. The addition features an observation area with a magnificent view of the sea. Wood, sea, and lush tropical vegetation are the elements that are combined in this charming hotel to give guests a rich experience of Jamaica.

jamaica inn hotel

Ocho Rios, Jamaica

Jamaica Inn is a forty-five-room hotel located two miles from Ocho Rios on Jamaica's north coast. The land for this establishment consists of more than six acres of terrain opening onto an inlet with a long strip of sandy beach. Each end of the beach is protected by a rocky point and a reef. This is a perfect place for diving, sailing, or windsurfing.

The Jamaica Inn is a historical reference for elegant society, classically Caribbean, comfortably equipped, and located only eight minutes from the coastal community of Ocho Rios. The inn has a long tradition as a retreat for the island's élite. It has been voted as one of the twenty-five best small hotels in the world by the readers of the prestigious magazine Condé Nast Traveller. This recognition has been endorsed by such illustrious guests as Sir Winston Churchill and Errol Flynn, who chose this small hotel to spend a few days of rest.

The interior decor is elegant and sober. In each of the forty-five rooms, sky-blue tones predominate, as well as turquoises and whites. These colors contrast with the green of the Jamaican vegetation outside. The private terraces of each room, with balustrades that have Classical columns, offer superb panoramic views. The restaurant has become famous for its excellent Jamaican and international dishes.

Detail of one of the gardens of the hotel.

View of the sea from the pool.

The rooms have private rooms all decorated in a colonial style.

The bedroom opens onto a terrace that is elegantly decorated
with printed floral designs.

Overall view of the pool.

k.club

Barbuda Island, Lesser Antilles

The Caribbean island of Barbuda is a small, solitary paradise ringed by
deserted beaches and nature reserves, such as the Grand Lagoon,
which shelters thousands of birds. Several years ago, the Italian
designer Krizia acquired the lands in this idyllic setting upon which
to build the exclusive K Club hotel. He entrusted the construction of
the hotel to the architect Gianni Gamondi, who had earlier carried
out spectacular projects on Emerald Island. The interior design was
entrusted to Mariuccia Mandelli. Opened in 1989, the hotel has a
modern floor plan crowned with a triangular apex. The 36
bungalow-style rooms and the nine suites are spread along the two
kilometers of beach, within an area of 230 acres which includes a
nine-hole golf course and two tennis courts. Between the beach and
the tropical garden, various common services have been set up for
the guests, such as a reception area, lounges, a bar, and a library.
The 146-column club house is the center of the complex.
It is defined by a large lounging area with wicker sofas, teak wood,
and an imposing patio complete with leafy tropical vegetation.
This space, which is decorated like the rest of the hotel in white
tones and turquoise, is divided into two levels, a large hall next to
the bar, for conversation, and a library for reading. The library, which
has diffuse, discreet lighting, is in the upper part, and connects to
the lower part by a white wooden stairway. Next to the bar are the
climatized pool and the jacuzzi, ringed by a perimeter of teak wood
with scattered palms. The decor of the bungalows is minimalist and
practical: wicker, natural fibers, bare walls where once again the
colors blue and white are seen in combination. Some of the
bungalows have a living room and two bedrooms with a central
patio. The bedrooms are ample (six by six meters) and the bathrooms
open up to the exuberant vegetation of the island. Each bungalow
has a kitchen and a porch with deck chairs and portable roofs.

Surrounded by a perimeter of teak wood, the climatized pool offers spectacular views of the sea and of the solitary beach.

The sober and subtle lines of the hotel are perfectly adapted to the tropical vegetation. The deck chairs in the photograph are by Balneis.

The club house, with its 146 columns, includes a large rest area with wicker sofas and teak wood furniture.

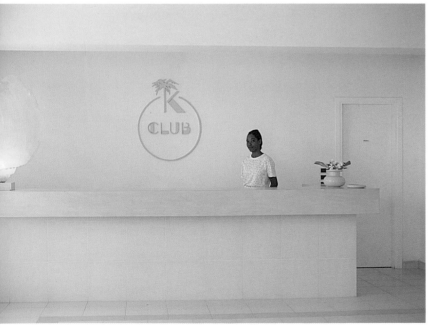

Turquoise and white tones are repeated in the minimalist decor. The reception area is uniquely defined by a large wooden counter with a lamp, a Savana Srl design.

The salon in a bungalow-suite, with wicker sofas, marine fabrics, and a small teak table. A coco rug has been used to protect the floor. The roof has exposed wood beams, painted turqoise.

From the beach of the K Club hotel, guests may enjoy the superb atmosphere.

bora bora Lagoon resort

Vaitape, Bora Bora

Bora Bora is located 150 miles to the northeast of Tahiti, and forms part
of French Polynesia's Society Islands. The hotel of Bora Bora Lagoon
Resort is surrounded by a spectacular lagoon created from the reefs.
The hotel offers lodging in luxurious bungalows next to the water or
among the gardens along the beach. Established in 1994, the hotel is
the creation of David Fleeting and the architects of the firm of
Hagues Tricard and Jean Picart.

The interior design was carried out under the oversight of Roger Pyke
and Yolande Clarkson, who also do two-year updates.

The site offers a nine-acre aquatica area with a private coral reef, from
which the sacred mountain of Otemanu can be glimpsed in the
northeast. A portion of the main building is set upon firm ground,
while the rest reaches out over the water. The primary recreation
area is located behind the central facilities, which include a pool,
platforms, and typical Tahitian entertainment areas. The tennis
courts are located in an area protected from the heat and sun by a
small stand of trees. The bungalows seem to emerge from the
lagoon, and their design reflects Tahitian tradition, with vaulted
straw roofs, bamboo walls, and floors of polished manioc. The guests
arrive at the reception pier, which is located to the east of the
buildings in the central complex. The chairs are made of dark,
densely woven wicker combined with magenta- and electric-green-
colored cushions. The circular sofa, covered in white canvas,
contrasts nicely. The library, called the Pavilion, provides an inviting
space for reading or conversation. This area is accessible from the
lobby and the restaurant, and is decorated in light-brown pastel
tones. At the end of the observation room one finds the Otemanu
restaurant, which actually floats above the lagoon. It has coconut
wood floors, chairs covered in natural hide combined with cane and
green and violet fabrics, along with tables made of Asian Jati wood.
These together define this as an enchanting place for enjoying either
international cuisine or dishes that are typical of the island.

Two natives on an authentic island boat bring a colorful breakfast nearer to the bungalow.

Contrasting blues in crystal clear water. A few bungalows rise above the water upon stilts.

Overall view of the pool. In the background, the white sand beach can be seen.

Thatch and bamboo roofs create the sense
of a typical island village.

Detail of the bath in one of the suites.
The blinds made of wood and cane
allow outside light to filter in gently.

Bedroom dressed up with polished yucca wood. Colorful fabrics in magenta, violet, and yellow lend a touch of color.

the sloane

Location: Chelsea. London

Address: 29 Draycott Place, Chelsea. London, SW3 25H

Capacity: 12 rooms.

Services: Business center manager, office support, translation services, courier, telecommunications and office equipment.

Season: Open year round.

Reservations: Ph.: +44171.581 5757.
Fax: +44171.584 1348.

the Lowell

Location: Manhattan, NewYok

Address: 28 East 63rd. Street. New York, NY 10021-8088. USA

Capacity: 44 suites.

Services: Restaurant (Post House),fitness center (Gym Suite), twenty-four hour concierge, maid service twice daily, individual climate control.

Season: Open year round.

Reservations: Tel.: +1212.838 14 00.
Fax: +1212.319 42 30.
e-mail: lowellhtl@aol.com

parador de granada

Location: Granada, Spain.

Address: Inside the Alhambra in Alhambra, Granada.

Capacity: 30 rooms.

Services: Room service, parking, guided bus tours.

Season: Open year round.

Reservations: Ph. +34(958)22.14.40.
Fax +34(958)22.22.64.

the Hiragiya-ryokan

Location: Kyoto, Japan.

Address: Oike-kado, Fuyacho, Nakakyo-ku. Kioto.

Capacity: 33 rooms.

Services: Traditional restaurant, jacuzzi, Japanese-style community bath. Room service.

Season: Open year round.

Reservations: Ph. +075-221.1136.
Fax +075-221.1139.

schloss vier jahreszeiten

Location: Berlin, Germany.

Address: Brahmsstrasse 10, 14193, Berlin.

Capacity: 40 rooms, 12 suites.

Services: Pool, two saunas, jacuzzi, steam baths, solarium, gymnasium, private park, physical therapy, activities for children, room services, airport chauffeur.

Season: Open year round.

Reservations: Ph. +(49-30) 895-84-0.
Fax +(49-30) 895-84-800.

san roque hotel

Location: Garachico, a port on the northeastern part of Tenerife in the Grand Canaries.

Address: Esteban de Ponte 32. 38450 Garachico.

Capacity: 20 rooms.

Services: Climatized pool, sauna, solarium, tennis, fishing equipment, boats for cruising along the coast.

Season: Open year round.

Reservations: Ph. 34 922 13 34 35.
Fax 34 922 13 34 06.

seteais palace

Location:	1.5 kilometers from Sintra, Portugal.
Address:	Rua Barbosa do Bocage, 8.
Capacity:	30 rooms, 3 suites.
Services:	Pool, tennis, horseback riding area, reading rooms.
Reservations:	Ph. +35 (01) 9233200. Fax: +35 (01) 9234277.

villa san michele

Location:	Fiesole, 12 miles from Florence, Tuscany.
Address:	Via Doccia, 4, 50014 Fiesole.
Capacity:	26 rooms, 15 suites, most with a jacuzzi.
Services:	Room service, minibar, lounges, restaurant, air conditioning, hairstylist, jacuzzi, free minibus service to Florence.
Season:	Open from March to November.
Reservations:	Ph. +39(055) 59451-59452. Fax +39(055)598734.

regent beverly wilshire

Location:	Beverly Hill, L. A., USA.
Address:	9500 Whilshire Blud.
Services:	Restaurant, Room service 24 h., shoe shine, Parking, laundry, Kindergarden.
Season:	Open year round.
Reservations:	Ph. +1-310-275.5200.

château tour des puits

Location:	Savoy, France.
Address:	73800 Coise Sant Jean.
Capacity:	7 rooms.
Services:	Private heliport connecting to airport, putting green, guided tours of the surrounding area. Guided activities including sailplaning, skydiving, canoing, kayaking, whitewater rafting, waterskiing, and offroad excursions.
Season:	Open year round.
Reservations:	Ph. (33) 47-928-8800. Fax. (33) 47-938-8801.

hotel ferme de la rençonnière

Location:	Crépon, Normandy, France.
Address:	Route d'Arromanches. 14480 Crepon (Creully).
Capacity:	42 rooms.
Services:	Horseback riding, golf, tennis, sailing.
Season:	Open year round.
Reservations:	Ph. +02 31 22 21 73. Fax: +02 31 22 98 39.

the point

Location:	Saranac Lake in New York, USA.
Address:	HCRI, Box 65, Saranac Lake, New York 12983.
Capacity:	11 rooms.
Services:	Room service, equipment for fishing and aquatic sports, golf, skating, downhill skiing, French cooking.
Season:	Closed for annual vacation from March 15 to April 15.
Reservations:	Ph. +(1) (518) 891.5674. Fax +(1) (518) 891.1152.

chewton glen hotel

Location: Hampshire, United Kingdom.
Address: Christchurch Road. New Milton. Hampshire BH256QS.
Capacity: 33 rooms, 19 apartment suites.
Services: Fishing, golf, sports club, indoor and outdoor pools, sauna, gymnasium, massage, restaurant, croquet, 24-hour room service.
Season: Open year round.
Reservations: Ph. +(44) (01425) 275341. Fax. +(44) (01425) 272310.

château roumégouse

Location: Le Quercy, in the northern part of the department of Lot, France.
Address: Rignac-46500 Gramat.
Capacity: 15 rooms.
Services: Restaurant, valet and room services, childcare, offroad excursions, horseback riding, and shopping.
Season: Open from April to October and for Christmas
Reservations: Ph. +056 533-6381. Fax +056 533-7118.

L'hostalet 1701

Location: Ampurdan, Gerona, Spain.
Address: Plaça Major s/n, 17254 Regencós, Girona.
Capacity: Three double rooms with full bath.
Services: Room for showing and selling antiques, breakfast service, lunches and dinners may be ordered in advance, bicycle and Zodiac boat rentals.
Season: Open year round.
Reservations: Ph./Fax.: + 34. 972. 30 33 3.

château plessis

Location: French region of Mayenne, 30 kilometersfrom Angers, near the Loire.
Address: Plessis, Mayenne, France.
Capacity: 8 double rooms with private bathroom.
Services: Central heating, restaurant, sitting room, dining room, 14 hectares of woods and gardens, balloon rides.
Season: Open year round.
Reservations: Paul and Simone Benoist, Ph. + 33-41 95 12 7.

réaux hotel

Location: Loire Valley, France.
Address: Chouzé-sur, Loire 37140 Bourgueil.
Capacity: 17 rooms, 4 suites.
Services: Room services, tennis, boat rides, piano, restaurant, golf 4 kilometers away.
Season: Open year round.
Reservations: Ph. +(33) 0247540. Fax: +(33) 0247951834.

Les terrasses

Location: Highway between Ibiza and Santa Eulàlia, Ibiza, Spain.
Address: Carretera de Santa Eulàlia, Km 1. Ibiza, Spain.
Capacity: 9 double rooms, one suite.
Services: Restaurant, indoor and outdoor pools, enclosed sitting room, dining room, library, barbacue area.
Season: Open year round.
Reservations: Françoise Pialoux, Ph. + 34-971-33.26.43.

hacienda katanchel

Location: Yucatan Peninsula, Mexico.

Address: Merida, Yucatan, Mexico.

Capacity: 40 double rooms, one main suite with private pool.

Services: Swimming pool, restaurant, game room, organized tours.

Season: Open year round.

Reservations: Ph. +5299.234.020.
Fax +5299.234.000.
email: hacienda@mail.mda.com.mx

Las brisas Hotel

Location: San José, Balearic Islands, Spain.

Address: Apdo. de Correos 83, Porroig.
07830-San José, Ibiza, Baleares.

Capacity: Six rooms, three suites.

Services: Tennis court, bicycles, guided tours, air conditioning, satellite TV, telephone, minibar, and safe.

Season: Open year round.

Reservations: Emmanuel/René,
Ph.: +34 971 80 21 93.
Fax: +34 971 80 23 28.
608 53 44 67.

Saignon Hotel

Location: Provence, France.

Address: Saignon, France.

Capacity: Three double rooms. Maximum hotel capacity is eight people.

Services: Garden/outdoor museum, full bath in all rooms, central heating, separate fireplaces, reading room, four art studios (three inside and one outside).

Season: Open year round.

Reservations: Madame Kamila,
Ph. +33-4-9082.50.50.

jake's place

Location: Treasure Beach, Jamaica.

Capacity: 8 cabins.

Services: Room service, tours.

Season: Open year round.

Reservations: Ph./Fax: +(876) 965-0552.
Ph. +(876) 965-0635.

hacienda benazuza

Location: Comarca del Aljarafe, 15 minutes from Seville, Spain.

Address: C/ Virgen de las Nieves, s/n.
41800 Sanlúcar la Mayor. Sevilla.

Capacity: 26 rooms.

Services: Pools, tennis , putting greens. Hunting, target shooting, and horseback riding nearby. Private heliport. Guide and limousine services, childcare, tailor, laundry. Bullring and private hunting grounds for wild Spanish partridge.

Season: Closed from July 15 to September 15.

Reservations: Ph. +(34-5) 570-3344.
Fax +(34-5) 570-3410.

guanahani Hotel

Location: Grand Cul de Sac Bay.
Saint Barthélémy, French Antilles.

Address: San Bartolomé 97098.

Services: Pool with jacuzzi, two private beaches, and two tennis courts, aquatic sports, boutique, laundry, evening shows, room service, hairstylist, beauty salon, concierge.

Season: Open year round.

Reservations: Ph. +(590) 27.66.60.
Fax +(590) 27.70.70.

el castell

Location: La Seu d'Urgell, Lérida. Spain.

Address: 25700 La Seu d'Urgell, Lérida.

Capacity: 37 rooms.

Services: Café, terraces with panoramic views, outdoor swimming pool, large yard, library, mountain bikes.

Season: Open year round.

Reservations: Ph. (973) 36 05 12.
Fax (973) 35 15 74.

k. club

Location: Barbuda Island, Lesser Antilles.

Capacity: 36 bungalow-rooms, 9 bungalow-suites.

Services: Climatized pool, beach, two tennis courts, sailboats, library, bicycles, diving equipment, TV and video room, massage. Connections to the airport on Antigua by private plane.

Season: Open from November 15 to August 31.

Reservations: Ph. +(268) 460 0300.
Fax +(268) 460-0305.

jamaica inn

Location: Ocho Rios, Jamaica.

Address: Ocho Rios, Jamaica, W.I.

Capacity: 45 rooms.

Services: Room service, scuba diving, tennis courts, golf, sailing, boat rides, windsurfing.

Season: Open year round.

Reservations: Ph. +809-974-2514.
Fax +809-974-2449.

bora bora lagoon resort

Location: Mobu Toopua Isle in Bora Bora.

Address: Motu Toopua, B.P., 175. Vaitape, Bora Bora, French Polynesia.

Servicios: Fresh water pool, volleyball, fitness center, jacuzzi, windsurfing, speed boat to Vaitape, boutique, underwater diving, land excursions, activities for children, fishing.

Season: Open year round.

Reservations: Ph. +(689) 60.40.40.
Fax +(689) 60.40.01.